Trouble in the Sand

Written by Helen Depree ▪ Illustrated by Jeff Fowler

One day at school,
the children started fighting in the sandbox.
Carlos stamped on Anne's sandcastle.
Anne threw sand at Carlos.
Then all the children
threw sand at each other.

3

Some children started to cry.
There was a lot of noise in the sandbox.
The noise got louder and louder.
All the children in the playground
came to see what was happening.

"What's going on here?" said Ms. Hardy. She looked angry.
"This isn't the way to play together," she said.
"All of you, get out of the sandbox and come into the classroom."

The children followed Ms. Hardy inside and sat on the rug.
"I want someone to tell me what happened in the sandbox," she said.
All the children started to talk at once.
"One at a time please," said Ms. Hardy.
"I can't hear you
if you all talk at the same time."
"We could make a list of all the things that happened to us," said Carlos.
"That's a good idea," said Ms. Hardy.

7

"What things made you unhappy in the sandbox?" asked Ms. Hardy.
The children told Ms. Hardy
the things that had made them unhappy in the sandbox, and she wrote them down on a chart.

Things That Make Us Unhappy in the Sandbox.
Children pushing.
Children throwing sand.
Children fighting.
Children stamping on castles.

"How can you all play happily in the sandbox?"
asked Ms. Hardy.
The children told Ms. Hardy
the good things they could do in the sandbox,
and she wrote their ideas on a chart.
"We can call them
'Rules for Playing in the Sandbox,'" she said.

"Next time you are playing in the sandbox,
you can remember all your good ideas,"
said Ms. Hardy.

Rules for Playing in the Sandbox
Play nicely with each other.
Be polite.
Help each other build things.
Make up games to play.

After that,
there was no more trouble in the sandbox.